MINI BOOK

A DOZEN A DAY

Technical Exercises
FOR THE PIANO
to be done each day
BEFORE practicing

by

Edna Mae Burnam

Includes Online Audio Orchestrations by Ric Ianonne

Speed • Pitch • Balance • Loop

The exclusive **PLAYBACK+** feature allows tempo changes without altering the pitch.
Loop points can also be set for repetition of tricky measures.

To access audio, visit:
www.halleonard.com/mylibrary

Enter Code
1774-1187-6409-5432

ISBN 978-1-4584-1612-4

WILLIS MUSIC

EXCLUSIVELY DISTRIBUTED BY

HAL•LEONARD®
7777 W. BLUEMOUND RD. P.O. BOX 13819
MILWAUKEE, WISCONSIN 53213

Visit Hal Leonard Online at
www.halleonard.com

A Note from Edna Mae...

The *A Dozen a Day Mini Book* is planned to precede the *A Dozen A Day Preparatory Book*.

In many years of teaching piano to the young student, I have found that there is a strong need for technical exercises right away, when they BEGIN their piano lessons.

In the past I have been giving my beginning students technical exercises by rote until they were able to read the notes in the *Preparatory Book*. Now I feel there is a need for the *Mini Book* to be used first.

The *A Dozen A Day Mini Book* is designed for use with any beginning method or series for either class or private instruction. The exercises are built on the first few notes the student is learning, so they will easily be able to read the notes in the *Mini Book*.

When a student has completed this book they will be ready to enjoy *A Dozen A Day Preparatory Book*.

A DOZEN A DAY

Many people do exercises every morning before they go to work.

Likewise, we should give our fingers exercises every day *before* we begin our practicing.

Do not try to learn the entire first dozen exercises the first week you study this book! Just learn two or three exercises, and do them each day *before* practicing. When these are mastered, add another, then another, and keep adding until the 12 can be played perfectly.

When the first dozen – or Group I – has been mastered and perfected, Group II may be introduced in the same manner, and so on for the other Groups.

Many of these exercises may be transposed to different keys. In fact, this should be encouraged.

EDNA MAE BURNAM

INDEX

PAGE

To my family

Group I

1. Walking

2. Hopping

3. Bouncing A Ball With Right Hand

4. Bouncing A Ball With Left Hand

5. Rolling

6. Arms Up And Down

7. Skipping

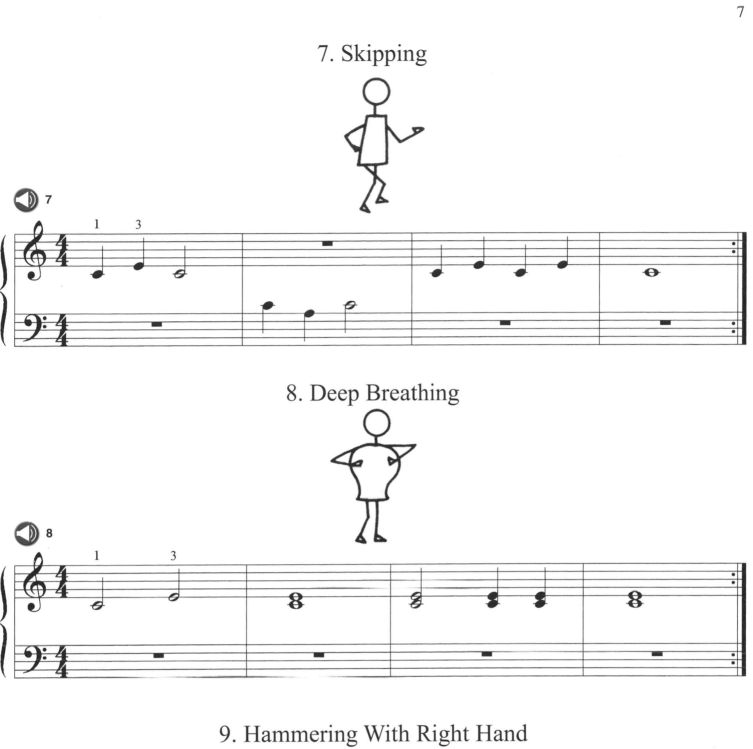

8. Deep Breathing

9. Hammering With Right Hand

Set thumb down silent.
Hold down throughout exercise.

10. Hammering With Left Hand

Set thumb down silent.
Hold down throughout exercise.

11. Walking In A Water Puddle In Boots

12. Fit As A Fiddle And Ready To Go

Now my fin - gers | feel so good. | I can play the | way I should.

Group II

1. Twisting Right And Left

2. Flinging Arms Out And Back

3. Touching Toes

4. Kicking Right Leg Up

5. Kicking Left Leg Up

6. Backward Bend

7. Stretching Legs Out And Back (sitting down)

8. Skipping

9. Deep Breathing

10. Jump Rope

11. Walking Down A Hill

12. Fit As A Fiddle And Ready To Go

Now I'm nim - ble   as can be.   I can play this   mel - o - dy.

Group III

1. The Splits

2. Deep Breathing

3. Wide Walk (Stiff-Legged)

4. Right Knee Up And Back (Lying Down)

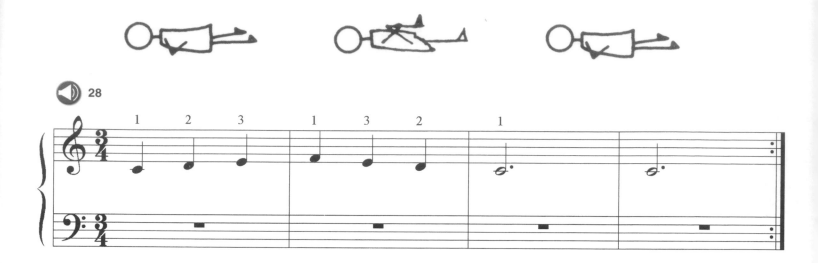

5. Left Knee Up And Back (Lying Down)

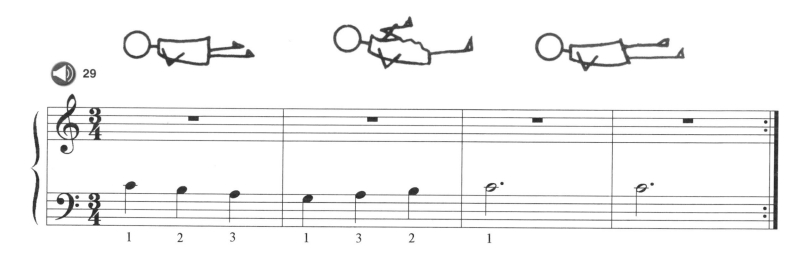

6. Both Knees Up And Back (Lying Down)

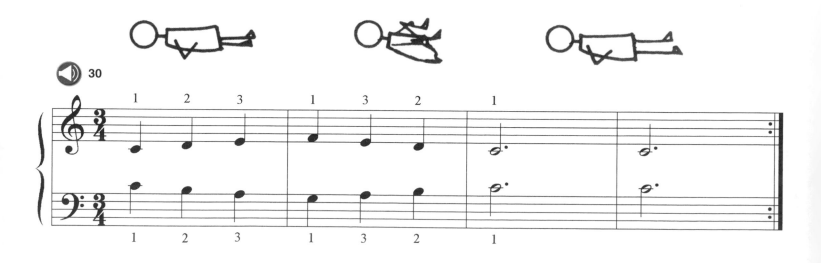

7. Backward Bend

8. Twirling To The Right

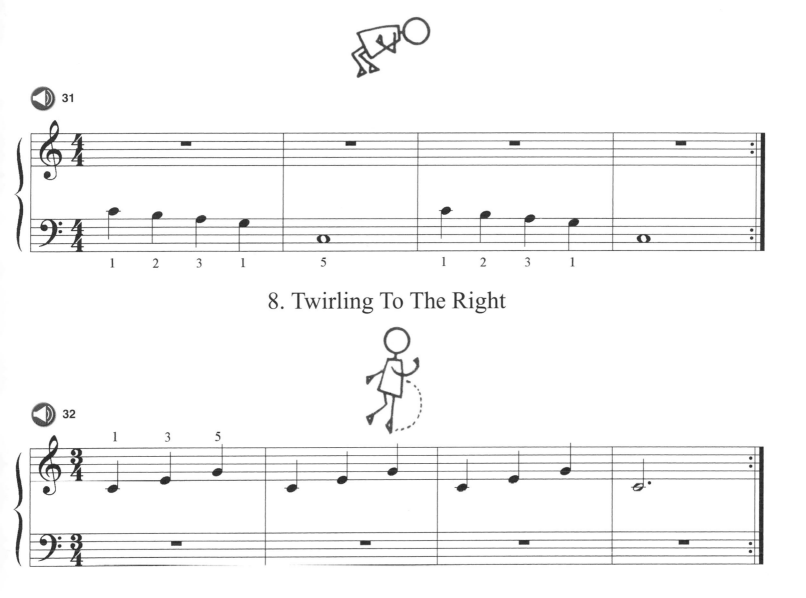

9. Twirling To The Left

10. Jumping Over A Bench

11. Jumping Off A Big Box

12. Fit As A Fiddle And Ready To Go

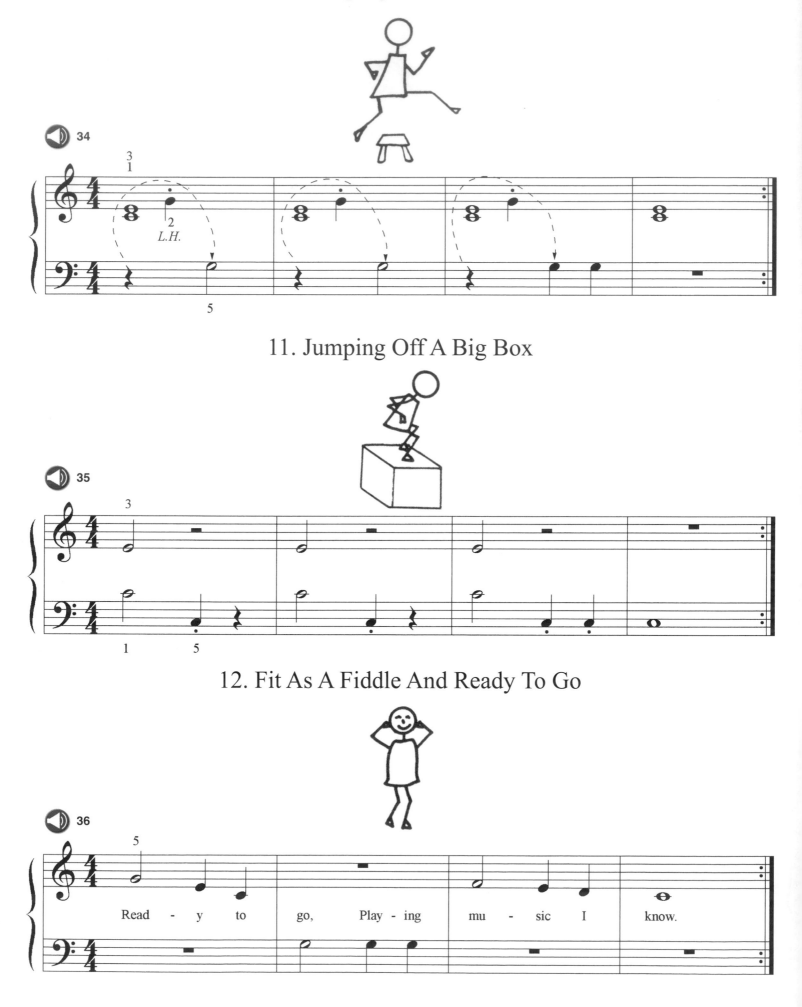

Read - y to go, Play - ing mu - sic I know.

Group IV

1. Walking On A Sunny Day

2. Walking On A Cloudy Day

3. Skipping On A Sunny Day

4. Skipping On a Cloudy Day

5. Deep Breathing On A Sunny Day

6. Deep Breathing On A Cloudy Day

7. Baby Steps

8. Cartwheels

9. Leap Frog

10. Tightrope Walking

46

Silent change.
Keep key down while
changing fingers.

11. Walking On Tiptoes

47

12. Fit As A Fiddle And Ready To Go

48

Fin - gers read - y as can be. Play - ing mu - sic just for me.

Group V

1. Running

2. In A Swing

3. Teeter-Totter

4. Whirly Gig Ride

52

5. Swimming

53

6. Going Down A Slide

54

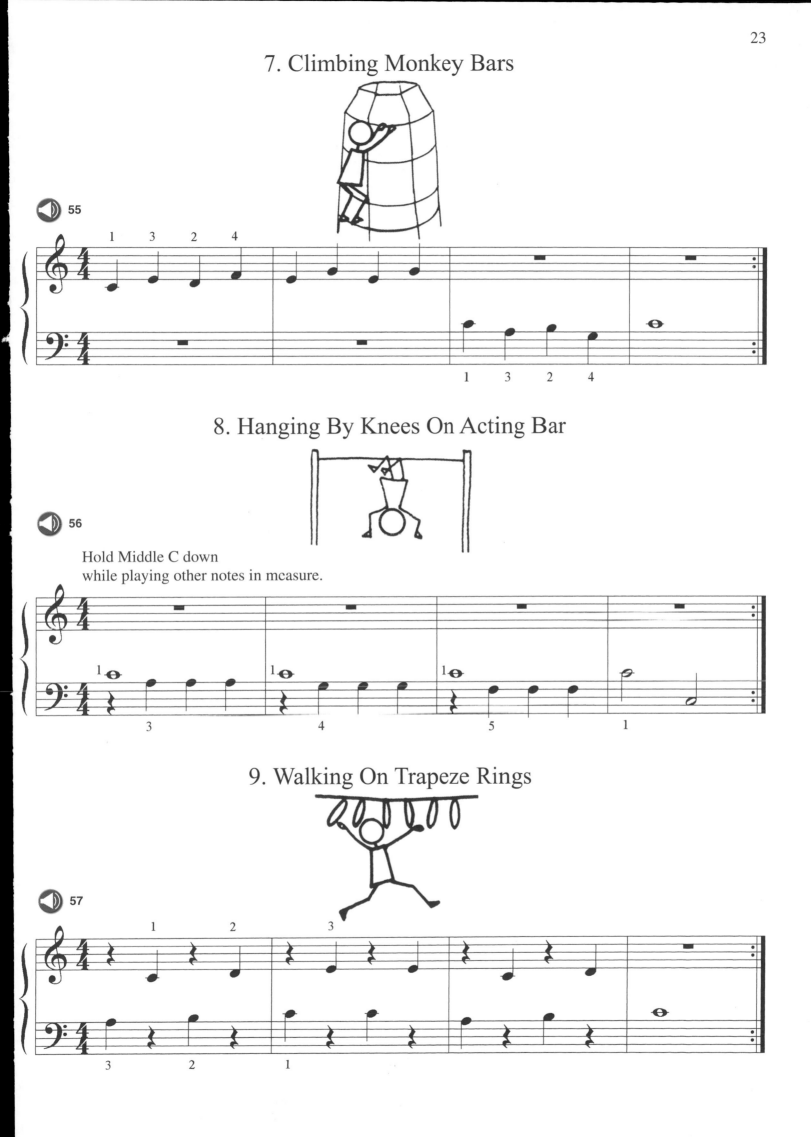

10. Jump Rope

11. Tether Ball

12. Fit As A Fiddle And Ready To Go

Nim - ble, nim - ble fin - gers | like to play | Lots of nim - ble notes to - day.___